# DRAMA CLASSICS

The Drama Classics series aims to offer the world's greatest plays in affordable paperback editions for students, actors and theatregoers. The hallmarks of the series are accessible introductions, uncluttered texts and an overall theatrical perspective.

Given that readers may be encountering a particular play for the first time, the introduction seeks to fill in the theatrical/historical background and to outline the chief themes rather than concentrate on interpretational and textual analysis. Similarly the play-texts themselves are free of footnotes and other interpolations: instead there is an end-glossary of 'difficult' words and phrases.

The texts of the English-language plays in the series have been prepared taking full account of all existing scholarship. The foreign-language plays have been newly translated into a modern English that is both actable and accurate: many of the translators regularly have their work staged professionally.

Edited until his early death by Kenneth McLeish, the Drama Classics series continues with his aim of providing a first-class library of dramatic literature representing the best of world theatre.

*Associate editors:*
Professor Trevor R. Griffiths
Dr. Colin Counsell
*School of Arts and Humanities*
*University of North London*

# DRAMA CLASSICS  *the first hundred*

*The publishers welcome
suggestions for further titles*

## DRAMA CLASSICS

# ELECTRA

by

Euripides

*translated and introduced by*
*Marianne McDonald and J. Michael Walton*

## NICK HERN BOOKS

London

www.nickhernbooks.co.uk

## A Drama Classic

*Electra* first published in Great Britain in this translation
as a paperback original in 2004 by Nick Hern Books Limited,
14 Larden Road, London W3 7ST

Copyright in the Introduction © 2004 Nick Hern Books Ltd

Copyright in this translation © 2004 J Michael Walton and
Marianne McDonald

Typeset by Country Setting, Kingsdown, Kent CT14 8ES
Printed and bound in Great Britain by Bookmarque,
Croydon, Surrey

This translation arises out of the work of the Performance
Translation Centre in the Drama Department at the
University of Hull, HU6 7RX

A CIP catalogue record for this book is available from
the British Library

ISBN 1 85459 749 3

**Performing Rights** Applications for performance, including
readings and excerpts, by amateurs and professionals in any
medium throughout the world should be addressed to the
Performing Rights Manager, Nick Hern Books, 14 Larden Road,
London W3 7ST, *fax* +44(0)20 8735 0250, *e-mail*
info@nickhernbooks.demon.co.uk, except as follows:

*Australia*: Dominie Drama, 8 Cross Street, Brookvale 2100,
*fax* (2) 9905 5209, *e-mail* dominie@dominie.com.au

*New Zealand*: Play Bureau, PO Box 420, New Plymouth, *fax*
(6)753 2150, *e-mail* play.bureau.nz@xtra.co.nz

No performance may be given and no other use of this material
may be used until a licence has been obtained. Applications
should be made before rehearsals begin.

## *Introduction*

### Euripides

There are three major tragic playwrights in fifth-century Athens whose works have come down to us: Aeschylus (ca. 525-456 BC), 7 of whose plays survive out of approximately 80; Sophocles (ca. 496-406 BC), with 7 plays out of approximately 120; and Euripides (ca. 480-406 BC), with 19 surviving out of approximately 90 plays.

The details of Euripides' life, based on information in the comic poets and later biographers, are unreliable. He is mentioned by name in most of the eleven surviving plays of the comedian Aristophanes, and turns up as a stage character in no fewer than three of them. One biographer states he was born in 480 BC on the day that the Athenian fleet defeated the Persians at the Battle of Salamis; another suggests that he lived his life as a recluse on the island of Salamis. Gossip emanating from Aristophanes implies that his mother sold vegetables in the market, that his wife was unfaithful to him, and that his secretary had a hand in writing his plays.

He certainly lived through the rise of Athenian democracy and seems to have become disillusioned by the manner in which popular opinion came to be manipulated in the Assembly. He was a friend and associate of philosophers and intellectuals and his plays often depict characters who are sceptical about traditional beliefs. He was wary too of false patriotism, and his plays are full of thinly-veiled criticism of the Peloponnesian War being waged against Sparta by his fellow Athenians, which dragged on for the last twenty-five years of his life and ended in total defeat for Athens soon after his death. This war produced a number of atrocities which Euripides may have castigated by dramatising parallel incidents in the mainly mythological scenarios of his tragedies.

Euripides is reputed to have spent the last two years of his life, until his death in 406 BC, in the north of Greece as a guest of Archelaus, King of Macedon, and it may be that he left his native city to avoid the horrors of the impending Athenian defeat.

Tragedy and Comedy in Athens were presented in competition at two major religious festivals in honour of the god Dionysus. Euripides won his first victory with a group of four plays at the Greater Dionysia of 442 BC. Probably as a result of his controversial subject matter, he recorded only three other victories in his lifetime from an output of some ninety plays. A further first prize was awarded posthumously for a group which included *Iphigenia at Aulis* and *Bacchae* in 405 BC.

Although in his own lifetime he was not as successful as Aeschylus and Sophocles, he became more popular than either after his death. Nineteen of his plays survive, more than those of Aeschylus and Sophocles combined, although this is in part due to an accident of history. He certainly appealed to later generations: many today find him the most 'modern' of all the Greeks.

Alongside his surviving tragedies is our only complete satyr play, *Cyclops*. Others of his plays, such as *Alcestis*, *Helen* and *Ion* have a comic touch and look forward more to the New Comedy of the following century than back to the savage dignity of Aeschylus. Indeed, there is more than one play in which he appears to make fun of the work of his predecessors. The dates of performance for eight of his surviving plays are shown in bold type below; others are tentatively proposed, on the basis of evidence provided by ancient writers, or of his own developing metrical practice:

| | |
|---|---|
| *Alcestis* | **438 BC** |
| *Medea* | **431 BC** |
| *Children of Heracles* | ca. 430 BC |
| *Hippolytus* | **428 BC** |
| *Andromache* | ca. 425 BC |
| *Electra* | 425-13 BC (most likely 420-416) |
| *Hecuba* | ca. 424 BC |
| *Cyclops* | (possibly in the same group as *Hecuba*) |
| *Suppliant Women* | ?424-20 BC |
| *Women of Troy* | **415 BC** |
| *Heracles* | ca. 415 BC |
| *Iphigenia among the Taurians* | ca. 414 BC |
| *Ion* | ca. 413 BC |
| *Helen* | **412 BC** |
| *The Phoenician Women* | ca. 409 BC |
| *Orestes* | **408 BC** |
| *Iphigenia at Aulis* | **405 BC** (posthumous) |
| *Bacchae* | **405 BC** (posthumous) |
| *Rhesus* | (undated, possibly not by Euripides) |

In addition, there are extended fragments of several other plays, in particular: *Antiope, Alexander, Archelaus, Bellerophon, Cresphontes, Cretans, Erechtheus, Hypsipyle, Captive Melanippe, Wise Melanippe, Phaethon,* and *Stheneboea.*

## *Electra*: **What Happens in the Play**

When Agamemnon returned home to Argos after leading
the Greek army which razed Troy and won back Helen,
he was murdered by his wife Clytemnestra and her lover
Aegisthus, Agamemnon's cousin. Aegisthus wanted to kill
Orestes and Electra, the children of Agamemnon and
Clytemnestra. Agamemnon's former tutor rescued Orestes
and took him to be brought up in Phocis, the area in
mainland Greece around Delphi. Clytemnestra persuaded
Aegisthus not to kill Electra, and instead Aegisthus
married her off to a poor farmer so that any children she
might have would pose no future threat. It is this farmer
who opens the play with a prologue, revealing that he has
had no sexual contact with Electra.

From this opening, Euripides takes his trademark
iconoclastic stance. Not only is his Electra both married
and 'unmarried' – the Greek name Electra means literally
'without a bed' – but she is living far away from the city
in a farmhouse close to the border. After the prologue and
an early domestic scene between Electra and her husband,
she leaves to fetch water from a spring, he to go and work
in the fields. Orestes arrives with Pylades, a friend from
Phocis. They hide when Electra returns singing a dirge for
her dead father. The Chorus of local women arrive inviting
her to a festival, but she declines and the two men step
forward to confront her. Though Orestes is by now aware
who Electra is, he conceals his identity from her and is
only revealed much later when the Old Man who saved
him as a child recognises him from a scar. For the present
he pretends to be a friend with news of Orestes and,
when the Farmer returns, he and Pylades are invited
indoors for a meal. The Old Man arrives, convinced by

offerings left at Agamemnon's tomb that Orestes must
have come back. Electra scornfully rejects the idea that
Orestes would be so secretive but the Old Man confronts
the two 'strangers'.

After Orestes is finally revealed to his sister, plans to murder
Aegisthus and Clytemnestra proceed. Orestes leaves and
kills Aegisthus while he is celebrating a feast for the Nymphs.
Electra asks for Clytemnestra's help, claiming recently
to have given birth to a baby. Clytemnestra arrives and
enters the house where Orestes is now waiting. Unlike
in Aeschylus and Sophocles, Clytemnestra's murder is
committed by Electra as well as Orestes, both their hands
on the sword. The details are revealed not by an indepen-
dent witness in the role of messenger, but by the
murderers themselves.

No aspects of the sordid and sorry tale are spared but the
play ends, as do many of Euripides' tragedies, with a
divine intervention which returns the story to its mythical
context while offering an ironic contrast to the reality of
the scene. Castor and Polydeuces, the demigod brothers of
Clytemnestra and Helen, appear above the action to
blame Apollo for what has happened. They tell Orestes
about the trial he must face in Athens and decree that
Electra should leave Argos and marry Pylades.

## The Historical Context

This is Euripides' slant on a story which was dramatised
by both Aeschylus (in *Libation-Bearers*, the second play of
the *Oresteia* trilogy) and by Sophocles. As the only example
we have of the same plot handled by all three of the
Athenian tragedians, the Electra plays are uniquely
valuable in comparing the differing approaches of the

playwrights. Though the Aeschylus is firmly dated to 458 BC, opinion still differs over the dates of the much later Sophocles and Euripides *Electras* and, notably, which is the earlier. Euripides certainly seems to draw attention to the version by Aeschylus, especially in his recognition scene between brother and sister. Sophocles and Euripides use the same title, *Electra*, but are so individual in their approaches as to suggest that either could have been a direct riposte to the other.

No firm date has been suggested for the Sophocles. The Euripides has raised some controversy. 'It is generally, and no doubt rightly, agreed that the Euripides *Electra* was produced in 413 BC.' So wrote the commentator J. D. Denniston in his standard edition of 1939, a verdict which arises from an apparent reference to the Sicilian Expedition in the speech of Castor. More recent commentators have questioned this, suggesting a number of dates from as early as 425, mainly on metrical and stylistic grounds, to 412, a date prompted by a belief that *Electra* could have been part of the same submission that included *Helen* and *Andromeda*, firmly dated to 412. The present authors differ on the dates for Euripides' *Electra*. McDonald follows James Diggle and Günther Zuntz, who claim new evidence indicates dates between 420 and 416. Walton believes, on dramatic grounds, that the Euripides was later than the Sophocles.

### *Electra*: Euripides and Realism

To anyone who knows Aeschylus' *Oresteia* and Sophocles' *Electra* – and this could have included many of the original audience in Athens – the *Electra* of Euripides is full of surprises. If the domestic setting in front of the house of a poor farmer provides the first, the manner in which the plot develops, the motivations and the way in which the characters address one another quickly dispel any preconceived notions of heroic or even revenge tragedy. It is not unusual in Greek tragedy for more homely characters to speak in realistic terms. Orestes' old Nurse in *Libation-Bearers* recalls changing Orestes' nappies. The Tutor in Sophocles' *Electra* gives a graphic account of a fictional horse race. Here, though, in the Euripides *Electra* realism invades the world of all the central characters as well as the more marginal.

Electra's relationship with her husband may represent an unorthodox and unconsummated marriage, but the Farmer gives a vivid impression of what it must be like to live with this obsessive woman. In their first exchange, he tells her there's no need for her to fetch the water. She insists that it is her duty, to which he replies:

Well, go if you have to.
After all, the spring's not so far away.

Later the Farmer invites Orestes and Pylades to dinner. She waits for them to go indoors before turning on him viciously for inviting guests who are above his station and when there's no food in the house. His grumbling response that a woman can always find something in the larder seems almost to invoke the world of domestic comedy.

Such prosaic exchanges have aggrieved some critics who have felt that Euripides demeans tragedy, but such a criticism assumes that tragedy comes in only one form. The variety of the plays of Aeschylus, Sophocles and Euripides suggests that for the Greeks there was no such standardisation. Dramatically, this more mundane dialogue can be extremely effective, paving the way for much more loaded remarks in a similar vein, as when Electra tells her mother as she goes in to be murdered to take care not to get her clothes dirty from the soot. There is no Euripidean tragedy that does not have its comic moments, however dark.

Commonplace language also has the effect of inviting a modern response to both character and situation. *Electra* responds to such probing. It does not take much reading between the lines to reveal the density of the dramatic action. When Orestes first encounters Electra, he thinks, because of her appearance, that she must be a slave. She talks of her shaven head and filthy appearance, the rags she has to wear (and moments later the fact that she has to make her own clothes!), her friendlessness and the wretchedness of her life. Most of this is self-inflicted. More, some of it is patently untrue, and both Orestes and the Chorus know it to be untrue. The Chorus have just invited her to a festival and offered to give her something to wear. It may be humiliating no longer to live in the palace, but this Electra is much less threatened than is the Electra of either Aeschylus or Sophocles. She even appears to get a perverse satisfaction out of her martyrdom.

Orestes, Electra's brother, a heroic, if troubled, avenger in Aeschylus, an implacable one in Sophocles, seems more concerned in Euripides with his own skin. He and Pylades try to stay close to the border so that they can retreat the moment Orestes is recognised. Once he has discovered who Electra is, and has checked to make sure the Chorus are friendly, he singularly fails to identify himself. In a play where so many other mundane questions are posed and answered, it is difficult not to ask why he is so unwilling to reveal himself to his sister. It is a question that actors and directors cannot avoid. Any answer reveals him as the most reluctant of assassins, an interpretation borne out after he is unmasked, in a scene which appears to parody Aeschylus' formal recognition in *Libation-Bearers*.

He is no happier about the sister he has found than she is to have him as her brother.

The Old Man has to tell Orestes where to find Aegisthus, while it is Electra who fiercely claims the right of killing their mother. When Orestes does manage to tackle Aegisthus, as a messenger reports, he accepts an invitation to the sacred ceremonial, asks Aegisthus for a cleaver and cuts him down from behind. In so doing, he betrays his role as guest and violates the ritual he was invited to attend.

It becomes clear that the entire play is fuelled by Electra's unremitting hatred of her mother. A factor in both Aeschylus and Sophocles, in Euripides this hatred appears less justified. In this play it was Clytemnestra who saved Electra's life. Familiar as we might be with Clytemnestra as one of mythology's villainesses, her portrayal by Euripides is sensitive and subtle. Her motives for murdering her husband are variously proposed. Electra's husband admits she had some justification for killing Agamemnon because he murdered their daughter Iphigenia. In his posthumous *Iphigenia at Aulis*, Euripides will take this further in a sympathetic portrait of a woman who brings her daughter, Iphigenia, ostensibly to a wedding with Achilles, only to find it is a ruse so that Agamemnon can offer her as a human sacrifice. Electra, on the other hand, accuses her mother of painting herself like a whore the moment that Agamemnon left home, and of rejoicing at news of any Trojan victory. Clytemnestra makes no attempt to refute this. Maybe the accusations are so wild she does not need to. Instead, she says it was Agamemnon's bringing back from Troy the mad prophetess Cassandra as his concubine that really made her want to kill him, an act she now regrets. Electra seems to be more concerned about being deprived of her status and inheritance than she is about her father's murder.

Whichever version one chooses to favour, Clytemnestra has responded as a mother to a request from a daughter for help after childbirth. She may seem shallow, weak or foolish, but she is not the monster Electra leads us to expect. Euripides is working his reversals, as he does in so many of his plays. When the Dioscuri, the heavenly twins Castor and Polydeuces, arrive at the end, they decree that Clytemnestra will be buried by Menelaus and Helen, who 'never went to Troy'. Euripides wrote a *Helen*, which was performed in 412 BC, based on this version of the myth which exonerated Helen from any responsibility for the Trojan War. Instead of deserting her husband and running off to Troy with Paris, the King of Troy's son, this Helen was whisked off to Egypt by the goddess Hera where she chastely repelled the advances of the local pharaoh while the Greeks fought their ten-year war for a phantom version of Helen. Clytemnestra may not emerge quite as guilt-free as Helen, but the process of rehabilitation is similar.

If Clytemnestra, Aegisthus and Orestes undergo something of a makeover here, everything feeds off Electra. Her husband recognises what she has had to face but that doesn't hide the realities of having to live with her. When Orestes says goodbye to her in the final scene, Castor responds somewhat sourly:

> She has a husband and a home,
> and doesn't deserve to be pitied.
> All she has to do is leave Argos.

This is a surprisingly damning verdict. It is the hapless Pylades who is then expected to give her a 'proper' marriage and reward the long-suffering Farmer.

The inevitable question arises as to why Orestes declines to reveal himself as soon as he finds his sister. Part of the reason he has come all the way from Phocis is to see Electra and enlist her help. Instead, he spends the best part of five hundred lines avoiding identifying himself. Clearly, neither brother nor sister is what the other was hoping to find. Orestes is hardly the angel of vengeance Electra had in mind, but then she is not what he was expecting either. The stage action that underpins these scenes may reveal all manner of subtleties in this relationship:

> You insult him, old man, if you suggest
> that my brave brother would return
> to this land by stealth for fear of Aegisthus.

So Electra tells the Old Man who has brought news of the lock of hair and libations on Agamemnon's tomb. Moments later, Orestes comes out from the farmhouse with no reason to expect that the one person who might recognise him has arrived. Even when the Old Man is introduced, Orestes still does not confess who he is. He says nothing at all between asking who this is walking round him, and the somewhat lukewarm response to Electra's 'I'd almost given up hope', 'It seemed so long to me too'.

If all this makes for a dearth of 'tragic' figures in any sense that would have appealed to Aristotle, it does create from a familiar tale a gripping horror story of savagery and near-madness. In 408, Euripides presented his *Orestes*, which takes up the story shortly after the conclusion of *Electra*, much as Aeschylus' *Eumenides* follows his *Libation-Bearers* as third play in the trilogy. The characters of *Orestes*, however, are not the same as their namesakes in *Electra*, though Euripides exhibits there a similar taste for the macabre and the unexpected. That play too ends with a divine intervention after Orestes has apparently murdered Helen and stands on the roof of the burning palace with a knife at the throat of Helen's and Menelaus'

daughter Hermione. Then Apollo tells Orestes that
Hermione is to be his bride! But this is how Euripides
wrote, a playwright with a sense of the absurd, driven, it
sometimes seems, to the edge of despair by the madness
which was dragging Athens down to its final defeat in the
long war against the Spartans.

## Euripides and his Philosophy

In Aeschylus, god can confront god and major questions
are raised about conflicting rights. Sophocles shows man
confronting god, fate and a world which can never be
entirely knowable. Euripides shows men and women forced
to confront themselves, and sometimes becoming the source
of their own defeat. In his universe, the gods can be
actively hostile to man. If Sophocles presents us with the
hero, Euripides shows us the anti-hero. According to
Aristotle, Sophocles claimed he depicted men as they ought
to be, but Euripides showed them as they were. Euripides,
who chose to be isolated from an active citizen's life, saw
things more bleakly than Sophocles did. It is difficult to
find or recognise any genuine heroes in Euripides except a
few brave women, or old men, or innocent children. The
main recourse man has in the chaotic Euripidean world is
to personal friendship. Heroism is dead, at least as it was
known to Aeschylus or Sophocles or, even earlier, Homer.

Euripides has been called the first psychological
playwright. Longinus praised his depiction of madness and
love. Euripides questions traditional beliefs and attitudes,
and most of his plays feature the kind of debates which
were popular among the fashionable philosophers of
his time known as sophists. These intellectual contests
bothered many critics in the nineteenth century, who
would have preferred inspired emotionalism without

philosophical discussion. Nietzsche condemned Euripides for just this rationality, which he considered a debasement of the noble goals of tragedy.

Aristophanes' *Frogs*, which highlights a contest between Aeschylus and Euripides, shows the latter as an innovator and iconoclast. It is from Aristophanes that we get the dubious idea that Euripides was a misogynist. He was, rather, a scientist of the emotions and focused often on unconventional, passionate women.

## Original Staging

The original plays of the fifth century BC were usually performed in the open-air theatre of Dionysus in Athens, which featured a circular playing area called the *orchêstra*. It may have had an altar in the centre. It was built into the side of the hill that culminated in the Acropolis on which the Parthenon stands. This theatre seated about 15,000 to 18,000 people, from a population of about 300,000 in Attica, comprised of male citizens, women, children, slaves and foreign residents. It is not known for sure whether women attended the theatre in Euripides' time, though they did in the following century.

The main Athenian dramatic festival was called the Greater Dionysia, in honour of the god of theatre, Dionysus. The Greater Dionysia was held in early spring, the 9th-13th days of the month *Elaphêboliôn* (March/April), when the seas were calm and Athenian allies and foreign traders and diplomats could safely make the sea journey. On the first day there was an elaborate show of tribute from the allies, war orphans were paraded, and prominent citizens were given awards. Going to the theatre was a social, civic and religious event. The city was on show, and the mood of the city was on show. One purpose of the festival was to impress foreigners.

Three or four days of the Greater Dionysia were devoted to plays. The performances began at first light and lasted all day. There are several plays whose action begins at dawn, or even in the dark.

Three playwrights were selected by a state official (*archôn*) in early autumn to put on three tragedies and one satyr play that comically handled tragic themes. This process was known as 'awarding a chorus' and ensured some state support and finance. The rest of the production costs were met by a kind of semi-compulsory patronage, known as the *chorêgia*, undertaken by private citizens. After the tragedians' group of four, political comedies, like those of Aristophanes, were played, either one on the same day as the tragedies, or several on a separate day simply devoted to comic performance.

Soon after Aeschylus began to present plays, a prize was given for the best tragic playwright and, later in the century, one for the best writer of comedy. The audience, who paid to attend, were closely involved with the performance and reputed to have openly expressed their feelings and reactions. The *chorêgos*, who paid for the costuming and training of the chorus, was also given a prize if his playwright won. The jury was selected, one from each of the ten tribes, but the winner was decided by randomly selecting only five votes from the ten that were cast. This helped to avoid jury tampering.

All the actors, including the chorus, were male and masked, playing both male and female roles. The masks were quite realistic but demanded a very physical kind of acting. Characters could be recognised by the audience from emblematic costume or properties. At first all the actors were amateur, and the playwright acted too. Eventually acting became professional, and prizes were then also awarded to the best actor at the festival, but the number in tragedy was usually restricted to three, possibly four, with doubling of many roles. In *Electra*, for example, the same actor may well have played the Farmer, the Old Man, the Messenger, Clytemnestra and Castor.

The chorus in Aeschylus probably numbered twelve but this number rose to fifteen in Sophocles and Euripides, twenty-four for the comedies of Aristophanes. After their initial entrance, the chorus usually stayed onstage until the end. The word *choros* means 'dance', *orchêstra* 'dancing-place', and their movements were accompanied by the *aulos*, a reed instrument (like an oboe), and sometimes drums. Spoken portions of the drama, mainly in iambic trimeter (a rhythm closest to that of ordinary speech), alternated with the choruses which were always in lyric metres and usually arranged in *strophes* and *antistrophes* ('turns' and 'turnings back').

Euripides' language in dialogue scenes is accessible, and at times colloquial, but he was a musical innovator and specialised in *kommoi*, formal sung laments for moments of heightened emotion. So popular were these that some Athenian soldiers imprisoned in the stone-quarries of Syracuse after the ill-fated Sicilian expedition were reputed to have gained their freedom if they were able to recite them. Euripides' choruses can range from being closely involved with the action and the characters to those that offer little more than breaks in the action between scenes.

According to Aristotle, Sophocles introduced scene-painting (*skênographia*) to suggest a visual background. Dead bodies could be displayed on a stage truck called the *ekkuklêma*, which was wheeled out from the central doors of the

building depicted on the *skênê* (backdrop, literally 'tent').
A *mêchanê* ('machine', or 'mechanical crane') allowed aerial
entrances and exits, usually of the gods.

In *Electra*, the Farmer's house, for all that Orestes and
Electra are so scathing about it, is more than some mud
hut even if it is unsuitable for the daughter of the former
king. It could have been suggested by the simplest scene-
building (*skênê*) and, perhaps, by painted panels between
the pillars of the façade to indicate that this was a rural
area. Similarly, country or seaside settings can be found
in Sophocles' *Oedipus at Colonus*, *Ajax* and *Philoctetes*; and in
Euripides' *Cyclops*, *Hecuba*, *Women of Troy*, *Iphigenia at Aulis*
and *Rhesus*. Entrances and exits along the *parodoi*, side-
passages which led out of the *orchêstra*, would indicate, on
one side where Orestes and Pylades have come from – away
from Argos – and, on the other, the Farmer's fields, the
place of sacrifice and the palace where Clytemnestra arrives.
The *ekkuklêma* would probably have been used for the dis-
play of the body of Clytemnestra, and the Dioscuri would
have been flown in on the *mêchanê*. The playwrights wrote
no stage directions, but we infer them from the dialogue.

The Athenian theatre was not a theatre of realism. The
playwrights did, on the other hand, make dramatic and
theatrical points about space, about status, and about the
public and private areas which were enhanced by a sense
of depth and height. Where characters go to and come from
adds immeasurably to the mood of almost all the tragedies
we have. Properties are used sparingly but tellingly.

## Performance History

Euripides' *Electra* has been produced rarely when compared
with versions of the same story by Aeschylus and Sophocles.
There was no modern revival at Syracuse until 1968, or

at the Epidaurus Festival until the following year. Gilbert Murray, in the introduction to his published version in the early part of the last century, described *Electra* as 'the best abused' of ancient tragedies. His translation in rhyming couplets was performed at the Court Theatre for twenty performances in 1906, and directed again by Lewis Casson with his wife and daughter, Sybil Thorndike and Ann Casson, just after the Second World War.

The play featured as part of the Trojan Wars sequences at Stratford East in 1964 in a translation by David Thompson and was subsequently performed at Chichester Festival Theatre. It was also part of John Barton and Kenneth Cavander's *The Greeks* for the Royal Shakespeare Company in 1979. Barton's production of *Electra* and *Orestes* had the eponymous figures, according to Michael Billington in the *Guardian*, 'turned into gun-toting Baader-Meinhof terrorists'.

Productions by Andrei Serban and Elizabeth Swados (in 1974), and Tadashi Suzuki (1995) were equally free in their interpretations. The directors revise and rearrange texts drastically. Suzuki's *Clytemnestra* (1983) combined Aeschylus' *Oresteia*, Sophocles' *Electra* and Euripides' *Electra* and *Orestes* into a composite Japanese text. His *Electra* was performed at Delphi in 1995. In Andrei Serban's *Electra* a snake figured prominently; the language was Greek, Latin and guttural sounds, only intelligible on an emotive level to most people: it was more musically percussive than textually comprehensible. In Suzuki's version, Clytemnestra returned as a ghost to kill Orestes and his sister who were locked in an incestuous embrace. Suzuki took much from Noh drama, and merged the traditions of East and West.

## A Note on the Text

This translation has been prepared from the Oxford Text edited by James Diggle (*Euripidis Fabulae II*, 1984).

Recourse has also been made to J. D. Denniston (edition with commentary) *Electra*, Oxford, Clarendon Press, 1939, 1954, 1960, 1964, 1968.

The manuscripts contain a number of lines which are difficult to account for except as errors of transmission. These have been bracketted in the translation.

Metrical lines other than the original dialogue in iambic trimetres are all capitalised.

Ancient Greek has various expressions of grief or dismay, *Io moi moi, Pheu,* and so on. The translators have chosen to leave these as transliterations from the Greek rather than translate them into English as 'Woe is me' or 'Alas'. The reader should accept them as sounds indicating dismay. Directors may choose whatever way they feel appropriate to convey the feeling behind the sounds.

Marianne McDonald
*University of California, San Diego*

J. Michael Walton
*University of Hull*

### *For Further Reading*

Christopher Collard, *Euripides*, Oxford, Clarendon Press, 1981.

Helene Foley, *Female Acts in Greek Tragedy*, Princeton, New Jersey, Princeton University Press, 2001.

Michael Halleran, *Stagecraft in Euripides*, London, Croom Helm, 1981.

Marianne McDonald, *Euripides in Cinema: The Heart Made Visible*, Philadelphia, Centrum, 1983.

————— , *Ancient Sun, Modern Light: Greek Drama on the Modern Stage*, New York, Columbia University Press, 1992.

————— , *Sing Sorrow: Classics, History, and Heroines in Opera*. Westport, Conn., Greenwood, 2001.

————— , *The Living Art of Greek Tragedy*, Bloomington, Indiana University Press, 2003.

Stanford, W. B. *Tragedy and the Emotions: An Introductory Study*. New York, Routledge and Kegan Paul, 1983.

J. Michael Walton, *Greek Theatre Practice*, Westport, Conn., Greenwood Press, 1980, 2nd ed., Methuen, 1991.

————— , *Living Greek Theatre: A Handbook of Classical Performance and Modern Production*, Westport, Conn., Greenwood Press, 1987.

————— , *The Greek Sense of Theatre: Tragedy Reviewed*, 2nd ed., London, Harwood Academic Publishers, 1996.

T. B. L. Webster, *The Tragedies of Euripides*, London, Methuen 1967.

David Wiles, *Greek Theatre Performance: an Introduction*, Cambridge: Cambridge University Press, 2000.

G. Zuntz, *The Political Plays of Euripides*, new ed., Manchester, Manchester University Press, 1963.

## *Euripides: Key Dates*

*NB All dates are BC.*

ca. 485/4 or 480   Euripides born

455     First competed at the Greater Dionysia

442     Won his first victory at the Greater Dionysia

438     First extant play, *Alcestis*, performed fourth in a group of four

431     *Medea*
        Outbreak of the Peloponnesian War

ca. 425 *Andromache*

? 420-416   *Electra*, the same story as handled by both Aeschylus and Sophocles

416     The sack of the island of Melos

415     *Women of Troy*

408     Left Athens for the court of Archelaus in Macedon

406     Death in Macedon

405     *Iphigenia at Aulis* and *Bacchae* performed posthumously in Athens. Featured as a character (now dead and in Hades) in Aristophanes' *Frogs*

404     Final defeat of Athens by Sparta in the Peloponnesian War

# ELECTRA

## Characters

FARMER, *married to Electra*

ELECTRA, *daughter of Agamemnon and Clytemnestra*

ORESTES, *her brother*

PYLADES, *his friend, nonspeaking*

CHORUS *of local women*

OLD MAN

MESSENGER

CLYTEMNESTRA

CASTOR, *a god*

POLYDEUCES, *his brother, nonspeaking*

*Various* SLAVES *and* ATTENDANTS

*A farm outside Argos, just before dawn.*

*Enter* FARMER.

### FARMER

Ancient land of Argos! Streams of Inachus!
It was from here king Agamemnon sailed
with a thousand ships to wage a war on Troy.
He killed Priam, who ruled the land of Ilium,
fabled city of Dardanus. When he came home,
he piled the barbarian spoils high in our tall temples.
There he was a winner. But here at home,
his wife, Clytemnestra, and Aegisthus, son of Thyestes,
laid a trap and cut him down.

Now he's dead.
The ancient sceptre has passed to Aegisthus,
who rules with Clytemnestra as his wife,
in this house of Tantalus.

When Agamemnon sailed for Troy,
he left behind a boy, Orestes, and a girl, Electra.
The old servant, who had brought up Agamemnon,
rescued the son, when Aegisthus wanted to kill him.
He sent him to Strophius to care for in Phocis.
Electra stayed in her father's home
where she blossomed into a young woman.
Suitors from the finest families in Greece
came to seek her hand in marriage.
Aegisthus was frightened she would bear a child

to avenge her father, so he kept her at home,
and turned them all away.

There was still the risk
she would bear a noble child in secret,
so he planned to kill her.
But her mother, savage though she was,
protected her from Aegisthus' cruel hand.
She might have killed her husband,
but she was still a mother . . .

This was Aegisthus' solution:
he offered gold to whoever killed Orestes,
Agamemnon's son, a fugitive from his native land,
and he gave Electra to me, as a wife.
No one can question my Mycenean ancestry:
I'm from a noble family, but I'm poor,
and poverty destroys nobility.
The weaker the husband the weaker the threat.
If he'd given her to a man of quality,
he might wake Agamemnon's angry blood:
then justice could follow and fall on Aegisthus.

I tell you this, the man that you see here
has never laid a hand on her.
The goddess is my witness: she is still a virgin.
I have too much respect for a lady of birth
to take her by force. I'm not her equal.
Poor Orestes, if he ever comes back to Argos
and sees his sister's sorry marriage!

If anyone says I'm a fool
to see a young girl in my house
and keep my hands off her,

then *he's* the fool –
with a dirty mind at that.

*Enter* ELECTRA.

### ELECTRA

Black night! Nurse of golden stars!
Pitcher on my head,
I go to fetch water from the stream.
Not because I have to, but to show the gods
How Aegisthus has destroyed us.
Into the vast wasteland of the sky
I send my keening for my father.
That murderous bitch, my mother,
Threw me out of the house,
As a favour to her husband.
Their brats have taken our place;
Orestes and I have become nobodies.

### FARMER

You poor girl, why do all this for me?
I've told you there's no need.
After all, you were brought up in a palace.

### ELECTRA

You are as good a friend as any god could be!
Never forcing yourself on me, amid my troubles.
It is great luck for someone to find a refuge
in misfortune, as I have found in you.
It is my duty to do what I can
to make your life easier
without your having to ask.
You have enough to do outside;
leave indoors to me.

When a working man gets home,
he likes to find his house well cared for.

### FARMER

Well, go if you have to.
After all, the spring's not so far away.
When it gets light, I'll take my oxen
to the fields and get the ploughing done.
Prayers without work won't put bread on your plate.

*Exeunt* ELECTRA *and* FARMER.

*Enter* ORESTES *and* PYLADES, *attended.*

### ORESTES

Pylades, best of men and a loyal friend
who shared his home with me,
you alone respected my situation,
when I suffered what I did from Aegisthus' crime.
Along with that murderous woman,
my mother, he slew my father.
After consulting Apollo, I have returned
to this land of Argos, in secret.
I shall repay murder with murder.
In secret, this very night,
I went to my father's grave, shed tears,
cut my hair, and offered the blood of a sheep.
I won't risk entering the city,
but will stay close to the border, with two aims in mind:
first, I want to be able to escape if recognised;
second, I'd like to find my sister,
who I hear has married, and is no longer a virgin.
I want to enlist her as an ally in this murder,
and find out how things really stand in the city.

Now, as the pale light of dawn brightens the sky,
we need to leave this public path.
If some farmer or serving-girl comes along,
we can ask if my sister lives nearby.
Look, there's a slave carrying a water pot
on her head; her hair's cut short.
Let's hide, Pylades, and listen. Maybe she'll give us
the information we have come for.

*They stand aside. Enter* ELECTRA, *singing a dirge, carrying a water jar on her head.*

### ELECTRA

Shorten your step with a song.
Walk on, weeping, walk on,
*Io moi moi.*

I am Agamemnon's daughter.
Clytemnestra,
Hateful spawn of Tyndareus,
Gave me birth.
'Poor Electra',
The citizens call me.
*Pheu, pheu,*
Endless pain,
And a hateful life.
Father,
You lie in Hades,
Slain by your wife
And by Aegisthus.

Come, cry the same cry:
Sweeten your sorrow
With a bitter tear.

Shorten your step with a song.
Walk on, weeping, walk on.
*Io moi moi.*

Unhappy brother,
Where, oh where
Do you wander, an exile?
You left your sister
In deepest misery,
Weeping in the rooms
Of her father's home.
Come and save me
From this pain,
Zeus, be our ally.
Avenge our father
For this shameful murder.
May the exile
Walk once more on his native soil.

*Enter a* SLAVE.

Take this water jar from my head,
So I may raise my nightly cry
To my father before the sun rises.

*Exit* SLAVE.

*Io moi moi.*

I sing a song of death
For you, father.
I sing songs of sorrow
To reach you below the earth;
I sing them day by day.
I rake my nails across my throat,
And strike my head now shorn,

While weeping for your death.

Tear your cheeks,
Tear your skin with your nails.
As the swan sings at the river's edge
For her dear father
Trapped in the treacherous net,
So I sing for you, father,
Washed for the last time
In a bath turned deathbed.

*Io moi moi.*

The axe's savage slash
Against you, father:
Savage scheme
On your return from Troy.
Your wife didn't crown you
With garland or wreath,
But greeted you with outrage
For the sake of Aegisthus,
To please her sly lover.

*Enter the* CHORUS *of local women.*

### CHORUS

Electra, daughter of Agamemnon,
We have come to your lonely farm
With the message that some Mycenean,
A reliable man, living in the mountains,
Has arrived to let us know
That two days from now
The Argives will celebrate a feast,
And all the unmarried girls
Will visit the temple of Hera.

### ELECTRA

No gold necklaces
Nor feasts for me, my friends;
They won't lift my poor spirit;
My foot shan't strike the ground,
No whirling dances with Argive girls.
I spend my nights weeping;
Weeping I spend my days,
A wasted creature.
My hair is filth;
I've only rags to wear.
Does this suit a princess,
Daughter of Agamemnon?
Does this suit Troy that remembers
My conquering father?

### CHORUS

Great is the goddess! Come on,
We'll lend you something nice to wear:
Rich clothes and gold to grace the banquet.
Tears alone won't conquer your enemy, will they,
Without honour to the gods?
You'll have good fortune, child,
Not through tears, but through prayer:
That's what the gods prefer.

### ELECTRA

No god is listening to me in my misery,
Nor cares about my father's murder
All those years ago!
*Oimoi.*
Grief for the dead,
Grief for the living,

A brother forced to wander,
An outcast in an alien land.
I wonder where he can be,
Living with nameless workers,
The son of a famous father.

Thrown out from Agamemnon's palace,
With grieving soul I wear my life away
Here in these bleak hills, in a peasant hut,
While mother lives with some other man
Wallowing in bloodstained sheets.

#### CHORUS

Your mother's sister, Helen,
Has much to answer for in Greece.

ORESTES *and* PYLADES *come out of hiding.*

#### ELECTRA

An end to weeping, friends.
Look!
Strangers by the shrine. They've been hiding.
You take the path. I'll try to get indoors.

#### ORESTES

Wait, don't run off.

#### ELECTRA

Apollo, protect me! Don't kill me.

#### ORESTES

I have enemies I'd much rather kill!

#### ELECTRA

Go away! Don't touch me. You mustn't touch me.

ORESTES

There is no one I have more right to touch.

ELECTRA

Why the sword? Why hide near the house?

ORESTES

Stay and hear me out. You'll understand, soon enough.

ELECTRA

I won't run off. You're stronger, so I'll listen.

ORESTES

I have news of your brother.

ELECTRA

O my dearest friend! Is he dead or alive?

ORESTES

Alive. I'll give you the good news first.

ELECTRA

Bless you, a reward for such sweet news.

ORESTES

A reward we both should share.

ELECTRA

Where is my poor brother forced to wander in his misery?

ORESTES

Your 'poor brother' must adapt to foreign ways.

ELECTRA

He has enough to live on, doesn't he?

ORESTES

A foreigner can survive, but he's powerless.

### ELECTRA

What message do you bring from him?

### ORESTES

He wants to know if you're alive and how you're doing.

### ELECTRA

Can't you see? I'm a shadow of what I used to be.

### ORESTES

I see you wasted by sadness and I sympathise.

### ELECTRA

With my head shaved.

### ORESTES

Distressed for your brother as well as your dead father.

### ELECTRA

*Oimoi.*
Who should I love more than them?

### ORESTES

Who do you think your brother loves more than you?

### ELECTRA

Beloved, may be, but he's not here.

### ORESTES

Why are you living so far from the city?

### ELECTRA

I'm married, but this marriage is a living death.

### ORESTES

Oh your poor brother. Your husband is a Mycenean, I hope?

### ELECTRA

Hardly the man my father would have chosen.

#### ORESTES
Tell me, and I'll let your brother know.

#### ELECTRA
I live out here in his house.

#### ORESTES
It looks suitable for a labourer or a herdsman.

#### ELECTRA
He's poor, but he's decent and treats me well.

#### ORESTES
What do you mean, 'treats you well'?

#### ELECTRA
He's never dared lay a finger on me.

#### ORESTES
From some vow of chastity, or does he not . . . .?

#### ELECTRA
He does it out of respect for my parentage.

#### ORESTES
Why wouldn't he be happy with such a wife?

#### ELECTRA
He feels Aegisthus has no right to give me away.

#### ORESTES
I see. Your husband's afraid of Orestes.

#### ELECTRA
That's true, but he's also respectful.

#### ORESTES
What a good man! He deserves good in return.

### ELECTRA
Yes. If my brother ever comes home.

### ORESTES
How could your mother let this happen?

### ELECTRA
Women put husbands first, not children.

### ORESTES
Why did Aegisthus treat you so terribly?

### ELECTRA
A weak husband means weak children.

### ORESTES
So no children to avenge you?

### ELECTRA
Exactly! I hope to pay him back for that!

### ORESTES
Does he know you are still a virgin?

### ELECTRA
No. We've kept this quiet.

### ORESTES
Are these women listening to us friendly?

### ELECTRA
They won't tell anyone what we say.

### ORESTES
What should Orestes do if he returns?

### ELECTRA
How can you possibly ask? Isn't it time to act?

ORESTES

If he does come, how can he kill his father's murderers?

ELECTRA

By daring as much as his enemies did.

ORESTES

Would you dare kill your mother with his help?

ELECTRA

With the same axe that killed my father.

ORESTES

Do I let him know that he can count on you?

ELECTRA

I'd welcome death with her blood on my hands.

ORESTES

Oh, if only Orestes could hear this!

ELECTRA

If he were standing here, I wouldn't recognise him.

ORESTES

Hardly surprising! You were both so young when you parted.

ELECTRA

I've only one friend who would know him.

ORESTES

The man who saved his life?

ELECTRA

Yes, my father's tutor. He's an old man now.

ORESTES

Did they give your father a proper tomb?

## ELECTRA

He got what he got, far from home.

## ORESTES

What you say pains my heart; men are moved
to hear of suffering, even if it's not their own.
You won't find pity in the ignorant,
only in those who truly understand.
But the wise may pay for too much wisdom.
Tell me what I must hear, however painful,
so I can know what to tell your brother.

## CHORUS

I'm eager to hear as much as you!
Living as far away as we do,
we don't get much news from the city.

## ELECTRA

I'm reluctant, but I'll tell you.
I'll tell you all the misery I suffer,
my own troubles and my father's.
Since you ask me, stranger,
I beg you tell Orestes about my degradation.
You can start with the rags I have to wear,
the filth that weighs me down.
Born in a palace, now look where I live.
I have to make my own clothes, or go naked.
I carry the water from the river.
Never a festival, never a dance.
With nothing to wear I avoid the girls.
And Castor, though related, wanted to marry me
before he joined the gods.
My mother sits on her throne,

Trojan spoils on every side,
surrounded by slaves my father captured.
Their fine dresses have clasps of gold.
My father's black blood stains the walls,
while his killer rides about in his chariot
brandishing the sceptre with which
my father led the whole of Greece.
His tomb is neglected:
no drink offering,
no branch of myrtle,
no bright gift of flame.
I've heard that,
when my mother's new husband
is drunk, he dances on the grave
and throws stones at his monument.
He has the nerve to attack us:
'Where is your boy, Orestes?
Protects your tomb well, doesn't he?'
That's how Orestes is insulted in his absence.
So, my friend, deliver this message, I beg you.
Many are the witnesses, and I speak for them:
my hands, my tongue, my crippled heart,
my shaven head, and our own father.
It's a disgrace!
His father took Troy. Orestes is young,
With a hero for a father, but he can't kill *one* man.

## CHORUS

Your husband's coming! I can see him!
He's left work and is heading for the house.

*Enter* FARMER.

#### FARMER

Now then, who are these strangers?
Why have they come to our farm,
so far from the city?
What do they want? A woman
shouldn't stand around talking to young men.

#### ELECTRA

Don't be suspicious, my dear. I'll tell you everything.
These men have brought me news of Orestes.
Strangers, I do apologise for my husband's words.

#### FARMER

What is the news? Is Orestes alive?
Does he still see the light of day?

#### ELECTRA

That's what they say, and they seem to be trustworthy.

#### FARMER

Does he still remember you and your father's past troubles?

#### ELECTRA

I hope so; but an exile has no power.

#### FARMER

What did Orestes have to say?

#### ELECTRA

He sent them to find out how I suffer.

#### FARMER

They can see for themselves; I'm sure you told them the rest.

#### ELECTRA

They know; I held nothing back.

#### FARMER

Why haven't you invited them in yet?
Please come in. I'll offer you the best I can
in return for your words.
[You there, take their stuff into the house.]
I won't take no for an answer!
You are friends come from a friend.
I may be poor, but I know what's right.

#### ORESTES

Gods! Is this the pretend husband
who refuses to shame Orestes?

#### ELECTRA

This is the man called poor Electra's husband.

#### ORESTES

*Pheu.*
There's no clear indication for man's inherent goodness.
Human nature is a random business.
I've seen the son of a decent man
turn out to be a nonentity,
and the best of children come from poor stock:
poverty in a rich man's judgement,
and a poor man with noble thought.
[How then can one make a clear distinction?
By wealth? That's not a good indication.
Or by poverty? Poverty is its own disease
and hardship can make men criminals.
By how he behaves in battle?
Who can judge another's bravery
when staring a spear in the face?
No sure answer for that one!]

Here's a man who's a nobody in Argos,
and has nothing to boast about his family,
a man of the people but he is noble by nature.
You who wander about with your heads in the clouds,
Make no mistake, but judge a man's nobility
by his character and how he treats others.
[That sort of man is a good administrator
in the city and in his own home.
But those big on brawn but small in brain
are only fit for the street corner.
In battle a strong man dies as easily as a weak one;
temperament and courage make the difference.]

It's right that I who am here accept this offer of hospitality
on behalf of Agamemnon's son who is not.
You slaves, go indoors. I'd rather a poor
but welcoming host than merely a rich one.
I praise this man's warm welcome,
though I'd rather your brother in his prosperity
were leading us into a prosperous house.
Perhaps he will come; Apollo's oracles are unfailing,
but I've no time for human prophecy.

*Exeunt* ORESTES, PYLADES *and* ATTENDANTS *into the house.*

## CHORUS

Now finally, Electra, joy warms my heart.
Perhaps your luck is changing
And your dearest wish will come true.

## ELECTRA

Idiot! How could you invite
these noble guests into our poor home?

### FARMER

What's the matter?
If they are as well born as they seem,
won't they be satisfied
with what we can offer, however meagre?

### ELECTRA

So, you invited them: do something about it.
Go to my dear father's old tutor,
now a shepherd, sent to live by the river
which divides Argos and Sparta.
Tell him we have guests,
and to bring food for a proper meal.
He'll be happy and thank the gods
when he hears that the child he saved is alive.
We can hardly ask mother for anything from home.
Discovering that Orestes still lives
would be bad news for that bitch.

### FARMER

If that's what you want, I'll go and tell the old man.
You go straight into the house
and make what preparations you can.
A woman can always find something
to add to a meal, if she sets her mind to it.
There's enough in the house
to fill their bellies for one day at least.

*Exit* ELECTRA.

When I think about it,
I realise that money has power,
to help you feed your guests,
or buy a doctor's help when you're sick.

But for day to day living, it makes little difference;
rich man or poor, once your stomach's full, you're full.

*Exit* FARMER.

## CHORUS

Famous ships
That once sailed to Troy,
With countless oars
Keeping time to the dances of the Nereids,
While the pipe-loving dolphin
Twisted and turned
Amongst the dark-blue prows:
You carried swift-footed Achilles
With Agamemnon to Troy
And the banks of its river Simois.

Nereids crossed the Euboean headlands
And carried the well-worked shield,
Golden armour from Hephaestus' anvil,
Up the slopes of Pelion,
Down the steep ravines of holy Ossa,
Where nymphs keep their sharp lookout.
Those nymphs spied him out
Where the horseman nurtured
That swift-footed son of Thetis, the sea-goddess,
As a shining light for Greece and for the sons of Atreus.

A man who came to Nauplia, a slave from Troy,
Told me there were designs
Etched on the circle of your famous shield,
On its outer rim,
Which struck fear in the Phrygians:
Perseus wearing his winged sandals
Skims above the sea,

And flaunts the Gorgon's severed head.
His companion is Hermes, messenger of Zeus,
Maia's child, fond of flock and field.

In the middle of the shield, the blazing sphere of sun
With his winged horses and celestial choruses of stars,
Both Pleiades and Hyades, shine in brilliance,
To dazzle Hector's eyes, and make him turn away.
On his helmet of hammered gold,
Sphinxes carry in curved claws
Prey seduced by their song.
On the breastplate that wraps his body,
The fire-breathing lioness flees on calloused paw.

On his deadly sword
Four-footed horses leap and prance,
Black dust swirling behind them.
Your lechery, vile daughter of Tyndareus,
Slew this paragon of spear-bearing men.
For this the gods above
Will punish you by death.
One day, some day, I shall see the blood
Flow crimson from your neck,
Slashed by the iron sword.

*Enter* OLD MAN *carrying provisions.*

## OLD MAN

Where is she? Where's my lady, my princess,
child of Agamemnon, whom I raised?
Whew! It's a steep path up to this house,
too steep for my old legs!
Still for friends I must drag along
my rickety legs and bent old back.

*Enter* ELECTRA *from the house.*

Oh my child, there you are!
Here I am! I brought you a lamb
from my flock, and cheese, newly pressed,
festive wreaths, and some special vintage.
Here, smell it! My very special treasure.
It's not much, but it will improve the poor stuff.
You there, take all this inside for the guests.
I can't see for tears. I have to wipe my eyes.

## ELECTRA

Why all this weeping, old man.
Remembering me at last, perhaps?
[The remoteness of this house, the rags I wear?]
Or does the thought of Orestes in exile upset you?
Or my father, whom you held in your arms as a baby
and raised to no avail for you and those you love?

## OLD MAN

To no avail, you're right, but I did do one thing.
I took a side path to your father's tomb
And, since I was alone, I dissolved in tears.
I opened the wineskin I was bringing for the guests,
poured some on the tomb, and adorned it with myrtle.
Then I happened to see a black-fleeced lamb,
its blood shed in sacrifice,
and, alongside, locks of blond hair.
I was astonished, child, that anyone had dared
go to the tomb. No Argive would.
Maybe your brother came in secret
and paid his respects to the pitiful tomb.
Hold the lock up to your hair
and see if the colour matches.

It's not unusual for those born of the same father
to share many physical characteristics.

### ELECTRA

You insult him, old man, if you suggest
that my brave brother would return
to this land by stealth for fear of Aegisthus.
Anyway, why should our hair match?
He of high birth, groomed in the wrestling ring,
I, a woman with fine-combed hair? It's absurd!
You can find lots of people with similar hair
who are no relation at all, old man.

### OLD MAN

You could try putting your foot into his print
and see if that matches, child.

### ELECTRA

A footprint on the stones?
But let's say there were one,
how would a brother's footprint match his sister's?
I'm a woman. He's a man with bigger feet.

### OLD MAN

If your brother does come,
isn't there something woven he was wearing
when I stole him away and saved his life?

### ELECTRA

I was a child, you realise, when Orestes left this land.
Even if I had woven something,
it wouldn't have grown bigger as he grew.
Some stranger must have come in secret to the tomb
and out of pity cut a lock of his own hair.

#### OLD MAN

Where are these guests?
I have a lot of questions to ask them about your brother.

#### ELECTRA

Here they come from the house; a well-timed entrance.
Their walk has a purpose to it.

*Enter* ORESTES *and* PYLADES.

#### OLD MAN

You can see they're high born,
but looks are deceiving.
Many of high birth are no good,
but I'll greet them anyway.

#### ORESTES

Ah, hello, old man.
Electra, where did you find this decrepit old wreck?

#### ELECTRA

This is the man who brought up my father.

#### ORESTES

What? The man who saved your brother?

#### ELECTRA

Yes. This is the man who saved him, if he is still safe.

#### ORESTES

Why is he staring so closely at me?
For some distinguishing mark?
Does he think he knows me?

#### ELECTRA

Perhaps he is happy to see someone of Orestes' age.

ORESTES

Orestes whom we both love. Why is he walking around me?

ELECTRA

His behaviour is peculiar.

OLD MAN

Lady Electra, my child, thank the gods!

ELECTRA

For something that exists or something that doesn't?

OLD MAN

This precious gift from the gods!

ELECTRA

Fine. I thank the gods. What for, old man?

OLD MAN

Look at him, child, the man you love most.

ELECTRA

I have been looking at him. Are you out of your mind?

OLD MAN

Am I out of my mind when I see your brother?

ELECTRA

What on earth are you are you saying, old man?

OLD MAN

This is Orestes, son of Agamemnon.

ELECTRA

What gives you that impression? What proof do you have?

OLD MAN

The scar on his brow. He got it when you and he
were chasing a fawn on your father's estate, and he fell.

## ELECTRA

What do you mean? Oh yes. I see the scar from his fall.

## OLD MAN

What are you waiting for? Kiss him.

## ELECTRA

You've convinced me.

*They embrace.*

It seemed so long. I'd almost given up hope.

## ORESTES

It seemed so long for me too.

## ELECTRA

I never expected . . .

## ORESTES

Neither did I . . .

## ELECTRA

Can it really be you?

## ORESTES

Your only ally.
If I throw the net right,
And make my catch,
I shall save you
From all your troubles.

## CHORUS

Dawn of day, long-awaited day,
You shine through darkness
And show the city its blazing torch:
He wandered for years in wretched exile,

Far from his father's house.
Dearly beloved lady,
It's some god, yes a god, who leads us to victory.
Clap your hands and shout out loud!
Pray to the gods, and with luck, blessed luck,
Your brother will walk the city in triumph.

#### ORESTES

Though your embrace is all very well,
we should postpone it until later.
You, old man, arrived just at the right time.
Tell me, how can I punish my father's murderer,
and my mother, in her unholy marriage?
Have I any friends I can count on in Argos?
Am I as short of them as I am of luck?
Is there anyone I should contact? Openly or secretly?
What path will lead me to my enemies?

#### OLD MAN

My child, no one in misfortune has an ally:
It's a rare friend who'll stick by you
in bad times as well as good.
Since you have no friends,
and no hope either, you'd better listen to me:
regaining your father's home and your city
rests in your hands and the lap of the gods.

#### ORESTES

What should we do to get what we want?

#### OLD MAN

Kill Aegisthus and kill your mother.

#### ORESTES

That's my goal. But how do I achieve it?

OLD MAN

Even if you wanted, you couldn't get into the city.

ORESTES

He has people on watch, does he? And bodyguards?

OLD MAN

Yes. He's afraid of you and that keeps him awake.

ORESTES

Right. So where do we go from here?

OLD MAN

Listen to this! Something just occurred to me.

ORESTES

Something helpful, I trust.

OLD MAN

I caught sight of Aegisthus as I was making my way here.

ORESTES

Ah, that's interesting. Where was he?

OLD MAN

In the meadows, close by, where the horses graze.

ORESTES

What was he up to? A bad start, but this looks promising.

OLD MAN

It looked like a feast in honour of the Nymphs.

ORESTES

For the children he has, or expects to have?

OLD MAN

No idea, but he's going to sacrifice a calf.

ORESTES

How many men with him, or were they all slaves?

OLD MAN

No Argive, just members of the household.

ORESTES

No one to recognise me, I hope.

OLD MAN

They were slaves I'd never seen before.

ORESTES

Will they side with us, if we win?

OLD MAN

That's how slaves are, fortunately for you.

ORESTES

How can I get close to him?

OLD MAN

Go near the sacrifice where he can see you.

ORESTES

Are these meadows close to the road?

OLD MAN

Yes. When he sees you, he'll invite you to join the feast.

ORESTES

The worst guest in the world, God willing.

OLD MAN

After that, you're on your own, as luck will have it.

ORESTES

Good advice. And where is that mother of mine?

OLD MAN

In Argos. She'll come to the feast when it's dark.

ORESTES

Why didn't my mother come with her husband?

OLD MAN

She was afraid what people would say.

ORESTES

Right. She knows that the citizens don't like her.

OLD MAN

Yes. They hate that godless woman.

ORESTES

How can I kill both of them at once?

ELECTRA

I'll take care of mother.

ORESTES

Very well, and good fortune will see you through.

ELECTRA

Let this man help us both.

OLD MAN

Glad to. How are you going to kill her?

ELECTRA

[Go to Clytemnestra and tell her this:]
Say I've given birth to a boy.

OLD MAN

A while ago or recently?

#### ELECTRA
Ten days ago, the time for ritual cleansing.

#### OLD MAN
What does this have to do with your mother's death?

#### ELECTRA
She'll come and see me when she hears I've given birth.

#### OLD MAN
Whatever for? Do you think she cares about you?

#### ELECTRA
Certainly. She'll weep at the child's circumstance.

#### OLD MAN
Maybe. So? Go on.

#### ELECTRA
When she turns up, she'll die.

#### OLD MAN
And she'll go inside the house?

#### ELECTRA
Isn't the road to Hades a short one?

#### OLD MAN
If I see her dead, I can die happy.

#### ELECTRA
Off you go then and take Orestes.

#### OLD MAN
To Aegisthus' sacrifice?

#### ELECTRA
Then go and give my message to mother.

#### OLD MAN
I'll tell it exactly as you said.

#### ELECTRA (to ORESTES)
Up to you now: you're the designated executioner.

#### ORESTES
I'll go, but I need to be shown the way.

#### OLD MAN
I'll take you, and willingly.

#### ORESTES (praying)
Zeus, god of my fathers, who puts my enemies to flight,

#### ELECTRA
Take pity on us, because we deserve pity.

#### OLD MAN
Pity those who are your descendants.

#### ORESTES
And Hera, Queen of Mycenae's altars,

#### ELECTRA
Grant us victory, if our cause is just.

#### OLD MAN
Grant that these two avenge their father.

#### ORESTES
You, father, now unjustly dwelling underground,

#### ELECTRA
And lady Earth on whom I lay my hands,

#### OLD MAN
Protect, protect your beloved children.

ORESTES

Come, bringing all the dead as allies,

ELECTRA

Your allies whose spears helped destroy the Trojans.

OLD MAN

And those who hate unholy pollution.

ORESTES

Father, who suffered so much at my mother's hands, are
you listening?

OLD MAN

Your father hears everything, but it's time to go.

ELECTRA

Everything. He hears everything.
But it's time for you to be a man.
[Kill Aegisthus.
I warn you, if you fail
to win that fight to the death
I'll be dead too – let no one think otherwise –
struck through the heart, with a double-edged sword.
I'll go indoors now and get things ready.]
If news arrives of your success,
the house will shout for joy.
If you die, it will be the opposite.
That's my warning to you.

*Exeunt* ORESTES *and the* OLD MAN.

You women, give a blazing signal with your cry
about this battle's outcome. I'll be waiting on guard,
sword held in readiness.
If we lose, I'll never let my enemies
avenge themselves on my body.

*Exit* ELECTRA.

## CHORUS

A story is told
Among all those old tales:
Pan, the lord of wild things,
Who blows sweet melodies
On his well-fashioned pipes,
Handed over a golden-fleeced lamb,
Taken from its unsuspecting mother
While grazing in the Argive mountains.
A herald standing on stone steps
Cried out: 'Come to assembly, to assembly,
Myceneans, to see the marvellous sign
That sanctions the god-blest rulers.'
And the people danced in honour
Of the house of Atreus.

Golden braziers were set out:
Fire blazed on all the altars
Throughout the city of the Argives.
A flute, Muses' help-mate,
Sang the fairest of its reedy strains,
But lovely counter-melodies
Filled the air and told
Of the golden lamb of Thyestes,
Who lured the wife of Atreus
Into an adulterous bed.
He took the portent to his house,
And announced to all the people
That he had the horned lamb
With its golden fleece at his own home.

Then Zeus reversed
The shining paths of the stars,
Driving the sun's fiery torch
And the pallid face of dawn
Into the west, to begin the day there,
With the blazing hot flame of divine fire.
Clouds pregnant with rain
Fled to the north;
Africa in the south became an arid desert,
Deprived of the fair rain Zeus used to send.

That's the story,
Though I don't believe it:
The golden sun
Reversed the course of his flaming chariot
To distress men
And make them pay for their crimes.
But these fearsome myths help the gods,
Encouraging their worship.
You forgot them, sister of famous brothers,
When you killed your lawful spouse.

Oh, listen! Did you hear a cry? It sounded
Like the thunder of Zeus below the earth.
Or did I imagine it?
There – the sound of voices on the wind!
Lady Electra, come out of the house!

ELECTRA *entering.*

ELECTRA
What news? How went the fight?

CHORUS
I only know I heard the cry of someone dying.

#### ELECTRA

That's what I heard, far off, but distinct.

#### CHORUS

From a distance, but clear enough.

#### ELECTRA

Was it an Argive or someone close?

#### CHORUS

I can't tell: it could be either.

#### ELECTRA

My death sentence; why wait?

#### CHORUS

Hold on till you find out for sure.

#### ELECTRA

It can't be good. We've lost. See – no sign of a messenger.

#### CHORUS

They'll be here. Killing a king is no small matter.

*Enter a* MESSENGER.

#### MESSENGER

We've won, women of Mycenae.
I bring news to all of Orestes' friends that he has won.
And Aegisthus, the murderer of Agamemnon,
lies dead on the ground. We must thank the gods!

#### ELECTRA

Who are you? How can I believe what you say?

#### MESSENGER

Don't you know me, your brother's servant?

#### ELECTRA

Oh dear friend, I was so terrified I didn't recognise you,
but now I do. What are you saying?
The hateful murderer of my father lies dead?

#### MESSENGER

He's dead. There, I've told you twice.

#### ELECTRA

Oh gods, Justice who sees everything is here at last.
Leave nothing out:
How did he kill Aegisthus? What stroke did he use?

#### MESSENGER

When we left here, we took the road
wide enough for wagons
until we found the new king of Mycenae.
Standing in the cultivated gardens,
he was weaving pliant myrtle for a wreath.
When he saw us, he greeted us:
'Welcome, strangers, where have you come from
and what's your country?'
'We're Thessalians,' answered Orestes.
'We're on our way to the Alpheus
to make a sacrifice to Olympian Zeus.'
Hearing this, Aegisthus responded,
'You really must join us for our feast. .
I'm sacrificing a bull to the Nymphs.
Rise early tomorrow: you'll still get there on time.
Let's go indoors.' He took him by the hand,
and said, 'Come, now, I insist.'

When we got inside, he told the slaves,
'Go quickly and get water for our guests

so that they can stand near the sacred basins.'
Orestes said, 'We've just purified ourselves
in running river water. If it is appropriate
for strangers to sacrifice with citizens,
Lord Aegisthus, we are ready and won't refuse.'
That's what they both said as they stood there.

The slaves laid down their spears
and busied themselves with their work:
they brought bowls for sacrifice,
and baskets; some lit the fire;
others set up cauldrons around the altar.
The whole room rang with the din they made.
Your mother's bedmate took the grain
and threw it on the altar, saying:
'Nymphs of the rocks, may I and my wife at home
sacrifice often to you like this; may we prosper;
and our enemies – he meant you and Orestes – fail.'
But my master prayed under his breath for the opposite,
that he regain his father's house.

Aegisthus took a straight-bladed knife from the basket,
cut the calf's hair and with his right hand
put it in the holy fire.
As the servants lifted the calf on their shoulders,
he slit its throat, then said to your brother:
'Thessalians boast they can do two things well,
cut up a bull, and break a horse. Take this knife
and show us if this is true or not.'

Orestes picked up the well-made Doric knife.
He threw off the fine cloak from his shoulders,
chose Pylades to help him in his work,

and pushed aside the slaves.
Taking the calf by the hoof, he stretched out his hand
and stripped away the skin to reveal the white flesh.
In less time than it takes a runner to complete a double lap,
he flayed the hide and cut through the flanks.
Aegisthus reached in and lifted up the holy pieces,
but the liver's lobe was missing;
the appearance of the portal vein and gall bladder
meant trouble for whoever looked closely at them.
Aegisthus frowned, and my master asked,
'What's wrong?' He replied, 'Stranger,
I fear foreign treachery. My worst enemy is
Agamemnon's son: he threatens my house.'
But Orestes answered, 'A threat from an exile?
You're afraid, you who are lord of the city?
Can someone bring me a proper cleaver
instead of this Doric knife to split the rib cage,
so we can feast on the innards?'
The moment he got it, he cut through the bone.
Aegisthus took the entrails, parting them
so he could get a good look. As he was bending over,
your brother stood up high and struck his backbone,
smashing his spine. Aegisthus shuddered,
convulsing in his final ghastly death throes.

The slaves ran for their weapons when they saw this,
Many men against just the two.
But Pylades and Orestes were brave,
standing their ground,
weapons at the ready, until Orestes cried out:
'It's me, Orestes, the wronged Orestes.
You served my father! Don't kill me!

I am no enemy to this city, nor to you, my servants.
I have avenged the death of my father.'
As soon as they heard this, they lowered their spears,
and one old servant recognised Orestes.
Then, shouting and cheering, they wreathed
your brother's brow. He's on his way here now
with a head to show you – no Gorgon's,
but that of the hated Aegisthus,
a bitter reckoning, blood for blood.

### CHORUS

Dance, beloved, dance!
Leap like a light-stepping fawn,
In joy approaching heaven.
Your brother has won a greater victory
Than in any Olympics.
Sing a song of victory
To accompany my dance.

### ELECTRA

Oh, light, gleaming brilliance of the sun's chariot,
Earth and night, objects of my former gaze,
Now I open my eyes to freedom
Since Aegisthus, my father's murderer, has fallen.
Come, my friends, search the house
For ornaments to adorn his hair,
So I may crown the head of my brother, the conqueror.

### CHORUS

While you get ornaments for his head,

*Exit* ELECTRA *into the house.*

We shall dance the dance the Muses love.

With the unjust now defeated,
Our former beloved rulers shall govern in justice.
Let our voices harmonise with joy.

ELECTRA *returns with ornaments. Enter* ORESTES *and*
PYLADES, *carrying the body of* AEGISTHUS.

### ELECTRA

Orestes, victorious son, son of the victor at Troy,
accept these garlands for your hair.
It is no pointless race that you have won,
but you have come home after killing Aegisthus,
the enemy who slaughtered our father.
And you Pylades, faithful friend,
son of the worthiest of men,
accept this wreath from my hand.
For you have won an equal share in this struggle.
May you always live in happiness!

### ORESTES

Thank the gods first, Electra,
the shapers of our fate,
then praise me, the servant of the gods and that fate.
I came and killed Aegisthus: not words, but actions.
And as proof, I bring you the corpse.
You can expose the remains as food
for the animals and the birds, heaven's children:
leave him skewered on the mountain.
Your former master is now your slave.

### ELECTRA

I have reservations, but I want to speak.

### ORESTES

What's the matter? You have nothing to be afraid of.

#### ELECTRA

I want to insult him, even though he's dead.

#### ORESTES

Do it while you have the chance.

#### ELECTRA

I want to, but fear holds me back.

#### ORESTES

Of what you might do, or what might be done to you?

#### ELECTRA

Of insulting the dead, in case I'm blamed for it.

#### ORESTES

No one would blame you.

#### ELECTRA

The city is quick to criticise, and enjoys it.

#### ORESTES

Say anything you like.
Our hatred for this man is unconditional.

#### ELECTRA

Right then. Where shall I begin, or end,
my catalogue of your crimes? What at its centre?
Every sleepless dawn, I've been going over and over
what I would say to your face if I were not afraid.
Now that's past, and I'm free to heap on you
the insults that I wanted to when you were alive.

When you deprived me of my father you ruined my life,
and you did this though I had done you no wrong.
You shamefully married my mother,

and killed the commander of the Greeks,
you who never even went to Troy.
You were so stupid you imagined
she would stay faithful,
though she'd betrayed my father's bed.
If a man seduces someone else's wife,
and finds he has to marry her,
he's in trouble if he thinks that she,
who has been unfaithful before,
will suddenly be faithful to him.
You were in hell, though you pretended it was fine.
You knew your marriage began in sin,
and my mother saw what an evil husband she had.
You were each as bad as the other,
and infected each other's lives.

All the Argives said this about you:
'She's the Queen, he's just the husband.'
It's a disgrace when a woman's head of the house
and not the man. I hate it when people talk of a child
as his mother's rather than his father's.
When a man marries above his station,
his wife is all-important, but he's a nobody.
Your biggest mistake was to think
you could do anything because you had money.
Money's nothing except a temporary friend.
It's character that lasts, not wealth.
Character stays with us through thick or thin.
Prosperity lives with fools who don't deserve it,
there a moment and then the flower's gone.

Then there's your women – no topic for a virgin-
so I'll keep quiet, but give you a hint.

You pursued women simply because
you lived in a palace and were so good looking.
I'd always prefer a husband with rugged looks:
no pretty boy for me.
A real man's children will be fit to fight,
not just to dance in a chorus line.

So much for you then!
You may not know how Time found you out,
but at last you have paid for your crimes.
Criminals should realise that
completing the first lap isn't winning the race.

#### CHORUS

He committed terrible crimes,
and terribly has suffered for them. Justice has great power.

#### ELECTRA

Very well, you there carry the corpse into the house
and hide it away so that, when mother comes,
she doesn't see it before we kill her.

*The* MESSENGER *takes the remains of* AEGISTHUS *into the house.*

#### ORESTES

Hold on! There's something else we must talk about.

#### ELECTRA

What's that? Soldiers from Mycenae? Do you see them?

#### ORESTES

No, but I do see our mother.

#### ELECTRA

Dressed to kill! She's walking straight into our trap.

ORESTES

What are we going to do? Murder our mother?

ELECTRA

Now that you've seen her, you're feeling pity?

ORESTES

*Pheu.*
How can I kill the woman who bore and raised me?

ELECTRA

The same way she killed our father.

ORESTES

Oh Apollo, damn you and your stupid oracle.

ELECTRA

If Apollo is stupid, who is intelligent?

ORESTES

He commanded me unlawfully to kill my mother.

ELECTRA

How can avenging your father hurt you?

ORESTES

I used to be innocent. I'll be exiled as a matricide.

ELECTRA

But you'll be guilty if you don't avenge your father.

ORESTES

I know that. But won't I be punished for matricide?

ELECTRA

Does avenging your father mean nothing to you?

#### ORESTES

Perhaps a mad demon spoke in the god's place.

#### ELECTRA

Sitting on a holy tripod? I don't think so.

#### ORESTES

I can't believe this was a good oracle.

#### ELECTRA

Pull yourself together and be a man.
Use the same treachery you used
to kill her husband, Aegisthus.

#### ORESTES

I'll go indoors. I'm set on a terrible course,
and terrible are the things I shall do.
If this is what the gods want, so be it.
But this is a bitter struggle, not a sweet one.

*Exeunt* ORESTES *and* PYLADES *into the house.*
*Enter* CLYTEMNESTRA *in a chariot and attended by*
TROJAN SLAVES.

#### CHORUS

I greet you,
Queen of Argos,
Child of Tyndareus,
And sister to Zeus's twin sons
Who live in the fiery sky among the stars,
Honoured as saviours of men
Who are tossed on stormy seas –
I greet you and worship you
As equal to the gods for your wealth and prosperity.

It is time for you to receive the attention
That your fortunes merit, my queen.

### CLYTEMNESTRA

Down you get, girls.
Take my hand and help me out.
The temples are full of Trojan treasure,
so I picked these slaves for me,
not much compensation for the daughter I lost,
but they look nice in the palace.

*The* SLAVES *help her from the chariot.*

### ELECTRA

Being a slave myself, exiled from my father's palace,
and forced to live in this wretched cottage, mother,
would you allow me to touch your blessed hand?

### CLYTEMNESTRA

Don't bother. I have slaves for that.

### ELECTRA

Why not? You kicked me out of the house,
and forced me to live like a prisoner,
ruining me and my home.
I'm an orphan like these slaves, fatherless.

### CLYTEMNESTRA

That's exactly what your father did,
scheming against those who least deserved it.
Now it's my turn to speak.
But no one wants to listen to a woman
who's lost her reputation. That can't be right.
Look at the facts: if it's right to hate, then hate,
but if the facts don't justify it, why would you?
Tyndareus didn't give me to your father

for him to kill my children.
But he lured my Iphigenia from home
to Aulis where the fleet was moored,
on the pretext of marrying Achilles.
There he laid her across a sacrificial altar
and slit her white throat.
Had he done this to save the city, or our own home
and the lives of our other children, one life for many,
it would have been forgivable.
But Helen was the excuse, that whore,
simply because Menelaus couldn't
keep his wife in line when she betrayed him:
that's the reason Agamemnon killed my child.
Even then, wronged as I was, I didn't run wild.
And I wouldn't have killed him.
But he brought back that mad priestess
to share our bed, keeping two wives in one house.
We're fools, we women, I admit it.
That being the case, when a husband
is unfaithful and shuns the bed at home,
the wife wants to do the same and get another lover.
Then they blame us.
It's never the men who are responsible.
If Menelaus had been kidnapped,
and Orestes had to be sacrificed to save him,
would your father have tolerated that?
He would have murdered me.
When he made me suffer the way he did,
how could killing him be wrong?
Yes, I killed him. I took the only course open to me,
and went to the enemy for help. What friend of his
would have helped me kill your father?

Your turn to speak freely, if you want:
tell me how your father died unjustly.

### CHORUS

You talk of justice, but it's a shabby justice.
A proper woman obeys her husband,
no matter what he wants. Any woman
who thinks otherwise is the lowest of the low.

### ELECTRA

Keep your last words in mind, mother:
you gave me permission to say what I want.

### CLYTEMNESTRA

I said it. I'm not taking it back.

### ELECTRA

So you'll hear me out: do you promise not to punish me?

### CLYTEMNESTRA

No. I'd really like to know what you think.

### ELECTRA

I'll speak then, and begin with a wish:
I wish, mother, that you had more sense.
Oh you're very beautiful, you and Helen,
I admit that, but you are two of a kind,
shallow and unworthy of Castor.
Helen went willingly to her own destruction,
whereas you killed the best man in Greece,
pretending it was for the loss of your child.
But people don't know you as I do.
As soon as your husband was away,
even before he'd ordered your daughter killed,
you were sitting in front of your mirror,

combing your lovely golden hair.
Any woman who dolls herself up
once her husband's left home
should be written off as a whore.
Any who shows her pretty face outdoors
is up to no good.
You were the only woman in Greece
to celebrate a Trojan victory.
If Troy was losing, your expression clouded over,
because you didn't want Agamemnon back.
Yet you had every reason to be faithful.
You had the man whom Greece chose as their general,
a man in no way inferior to Aegisthus.
When Helen behaved as she did,
this was your chance to shine:
a bad example is a warning for the virtuous.
Let's say father killed your daughter,
but what did I and my brother ever do to hurt you?
After you killed him why didn't you
give us the palace, instead of handing what wasn't yours
to a husband you bought with this dowry?
Why isn't Aegisthus in exile instead of Orestes?
Why hasn't Aegisthus' life been ended,
the way you ended mine,
in a living death twice as bad as my sister's?
If blood is paid with blood, then I and your boy Orestes
will kill you to avenge our father.
If what you did was just, this would also be just.
[Anyone who marries a bad woman
for her wealth and status, is a fool;
better a good wife who's poor
than a bad one even if she's wealthy.

### CHORUS

You never know with marriages: some turn out well,
some badly. That's the way I see it.]

### CLYTEMNESTRA

You've always loved your father best, my child.
But that's how it is. Some children prefer men,
others love their mother more than their father.
I forgive you for that. And I'm not proud
of some of the things that I have done . . .
All that plotting has only made me miserable.
That anger against my husband was too much.

### ELECTRA

It's a bit late for remorse.
No cure now: my father's dead.
Why don't you bring back your homeless son?

### CLYTEMNESTRA

I'm frightened, for my own sake not his.
I hear he's still angry about his father's murder.

### ELECTRA

Why do you put up with your husband's abusing me?

### CLYTEMNESTRA

Oh, that's just his way. You're pretty stubborn yourself.

### ELECTRA

It hurts me, but my anger will pass.

### CLYTEMNESTRA

Then he won't be so hard on you.

### ELECTRA

He's a social climber: he's there in my house.

## CLYTEMNESTRA

See what you do! You can't leave it can you?

## ELECTRA

I'll keep quiet. I fear him as much as he deserves.

## CLYTEMNESTRA

That's enough. Why did you send for me, child?

## ELECTRA

I think you've heard I had a baby.
Please perform the sacrifice that ritual requires
ten nights after its birth: I don't know how to do it.
I've no experience. I've never had a child before.

## CLYTEMNESTRA

That's a job for the midwife.

## ELECTRA

I had to be my own midwife.

## CLYTEMNESTRA

Don't you have any friendly neighbours?

## ELECTRA

No one wants beggars for friends.

## CLYTEMNESTRA

You're so dirty and dressed in rags:
and you've just given birth to a child!
So, I'll perform the appropriate sacrifice for you,
and after that I'll go to join my husband.
He's in the field making an offering to the Nymphs.

Slaves, take this carriage away and give the horses some hay.
When you think I've finished this ritual for the gods,
come back. I must do something for my husband.

## ELECTRA

Go into my poor house, but take care
not to dirty your clothes from the soot.

*Exit* CLYTEMNESTRA *into the house. The* SERVANTS
*remove the chariot.*

You'll make the sacrifice the gods want.
The basket's ready, the knife sharpened,
the one that killed the bull,
and you'll soon be lying next to him, struck down.
You'll be bride to Aegisthus in the underworld,
whose bed you shared in life. I grant you this one favour,
and you'll pay me back for my father.

## CHORUS

There is a payback for crimes.
The winds of this house have changed.
Once my lord, my leader, fell struck in his bath:
The stony roof echoed with his cries:
'Oh cursed woman, why do you kill me
On my return to my beloved land
After ten years of harvests?'

<                                                    >

The tide of justice turns, punishing her
For her love without law.
She raised an axe
To kill her poor husband,
When he finally returned to his home
Made with Cyclopean walls reaching to heaven.
Unhappy husband!
Whatever evil possessed that cruel woman?
Like a lioness roaming the mountain glades
She seized her victim.

### CLYTEMNESTRA *(from within)*

*Io moi moi.*

### CHORUS

Do you hear a scream from the house?

### CLYTEMNESTRA

Children, for the gods' sake, don't kill your mother.

### CHORUS

I sing sorrow because your children slay you.
God dispenses justice in his own time:
you suffered terribly, but your crimes
against your husband, cruel woman, were evil.

But here they come out of the house,
Covered with blood fresh from their mother's murder.

> *Enter* ELECTRA, ORESTES *and* PYLADES *followed
> by the ekkuklêma wheeled out with the corpses of*
> CLYTEMNESTRA *and* AEGISTHUS.

Here are visible trophies of those terrible screams.
There is no house, nor was there ever one,
more pitiful than that of Tantalus.

### ORESTES

Earth and Zeus who witness all that men do,
see this filthy work of murder.
Two bodies lying on the ground,
struck by my hand to repay
what we have suffered.

### ELECTRA

A sight too full of tears, brother, but I'm to blame.
I was cruel and blazed with hatred
against the mother who bore me.

## CHORUS

A bitter fate, a fate that made you suffer.
Mother of sorrows!
Unrelenting pain and more,
All at the hands of your children.
But you deserved it for killing their father.

## ORESTES

Phoebus, you foretold a dark justice, all too dark,
But clear enough was the woe that you wrought.
You made me a murderer, forced to flee Greece.
For what city here would take me in?
What god-fearing man would dare look on me,
A man who killed his mother?

## ELECTRA

*Io moi moi.*
What dance, what marriage can ever be mine?
Who would ever take me to bed as his bride?

## CHORUS

Your mind is as light as the breeze,
Blowing here, and blowing there.
You fear god now, but not earlier
When you persuaded Orestes
To do these terrible things
He never wanted to do.

## ORESTES

Did you see how the poor woman bared her breast
As we were killing her?
*Io moi.*
Sprawled on the ground the limbs that gave me birth.
I nearly fainted.

## CHORUS

I know what you must have suffered
When you heard the agonised cry
Of the mother who bore you.

## ORESTES

As she cried out, she put her hand on my chin
'My child, I beg you . . . '
She touched my cheek,
And the weapon slipped from my hand.

## CHORUS

The poor woman! How could you bear to look
At your dying mother,
As she breathed away her life?

## ORESTES

I covered my eyes with my cloak,
Thrust the sword through her neck
And put my mother to death.

## ELECTRA

I urged you on.
My hand was on the sword with yours.
Most terrible of all, I drove it home.

## ORESTES

Take this, cover our mother's body
And wipe her wounds.
Poor woman, to give birth to your own murderers.

ELECTRA *covers the body.*

## ELECTRA

See, I embrace your body with this cloth,

You who were both loved, and hated.
This is the climax of our house's great miseries.

*The* DIOSCURI, CASTOR *and* POLYDEUCES, *appear
on the mêchanê.*

#### CHORUS
Who are they, there, hovering over the roof?
Divine spirits, or heavenly gods?
That's no place for mortals.
Why are they appearing to us?

#### CASTOR
Son of Agamemnon, listen to me.
The heavenly twins, brothers of your mother,
Castor and his brother Polydeuces, call to you.
We've come from saving ships in a terrible storm,
when we saw you killing our sister, your mother.
She may have deserved death, but not at your hands.
Apollo, yes, Apollo, he's our lord, so I'll stay silent.
He's wise of course, but this prophecy wasn't.
What's done is done, and now you must live
with the consequences, as Fate and Zeus require.
Give Electra to Pylades to take home as his wife.
You leave Argos. You mustn't walk in the city.
A matricide would be unwelcome here.
Those goddesses of vengeance with dog-faces
will hound you into errant madness.
Go to Athens and throw your arms
around the holy statue of Pallas Athena.
She'll hold her Gorgon shield over your head
and she won't let them touch you,
though their snakes writhe in fury.

You'll find the hill of Ares there,
where the gods first held a murder trial
when, angered by his daughter's unholy rape,
savage Ares killed Halirrhothius, son of Poseidon.
From that time on this has been the place
of the most honest and secure trial by jury.
Here you must be tried for murder.
If the votes are equal, you will escape the death penalty.
Apollo who ordered you to kill your mother
will take responsibility for it.
This ruling will be set for all time:
'Equal votes acquit the defendant.'
The dreaded goddesses, overcome with anguish
at this decision, will sink down into a chasm
in the earth near this very hill,
and become a holy oracle for men of piety.
Then you must found a city in Arcadia
by the streams of the river Alpheus,
near the shrine of Lycaean Zeus,
and name it after yourself.

That's all I have to say to you. The citizens of Argos
will cover up the body of Aegisthus in a grave.
Menelaus, just arrived at Nauplion with Helen,
after the sack of Troy, will bury your mother.
Helen has returned from the house of Proteus in Egypt:
she never went to Troy.
Zeus instead sent a likeness of Helen to Troy,
to stir up fighting and slaughter of men.

Now Pylades, take Electra, both married and virgin,
as your wife. Leave the land of the Achaeans
and return to your home in Phocis,

with the man they call Orestes' brother-in-law,
and load him up with gold.

You, Orestes, must cross the Isthmus on foot,
and go to the hill of Cecrops, blest by the gods.
Once you have fulfilled the fate this murder imposed,
you will be happy, and your troubles will be over.

#### CHORUS
Child of Zeus, is it permitted for us
to exchange a word or two with you?

#### CASTOR
It is permitted. Murder has not polluted you.

#### CHORUS
Since you are gods and brothers of the dead woman,
why didn't you keep the Furies away from this house?

#### CASTOR
What must be must be, because of Fate,
Necessity, and Apollo's unwise words.

#### ELECTRA
May I say something too, divine twins?

#### CASTOR
You may. I blame Apollo for this bloody business.

#### ELECTRA
What Apollo, what oracles ordained
that I should be my mother's murderer?

#### CASTOR
You shared the deed and a common fate,
one and the same;
the same curse from your ancestors crushed you both.

## ORESTES

Sister, after years of separation, I finally see you,
yet straight away I am severed from your love.
I shall leave and be left in turn.

## CASTOR

She has a husband and a home,
and doesn't deserve to be pitied.
All she has to do is leave Argos.

## ELECTRA

Is there anything worse than leaving one's own country?

## ORESTES

I not only have to leave my father's home,
but must submit to the votes of strangers
in a trial for murdering my mother.

## CASTOR

It's not as bad as that. You are going to
Athena's holy city. Just do it!

## ELECTRA

Embrace me, dearest brother.
Our mother's murderous curses
are driving us both from our father's palace.

## ORESTES

Come to my arms; hold me close.
Mourn me as if I were dead.

## CASTOR

*Pheu pheu.*
Terrible for you to bear;
terrible words for the gods to hear:
the gods do feel pity for man's sufferings.

### ORESTES

I shall never see you again.

### ELECTRA

Nor I you.

### ORESTES

These are my last words to you.

### ELECTRA

Goodbye city,
and farewell to you, women who live here.

### ORESTES

Dear loyal sister, are you leaving now?

### ELECTRA

I go with tender eyes wet with tears.

### ORESTES

Pylades, go with my good wishes
and marry Electra.

### CASTOR

They'll see to their marriage. But you
flee the hounds and get to Athens:
those snake-fingered Furies, black in skin,
are hot on your trail,
eager for their harvest of fierce pain.
We must hurry away
to save ships on a Sicilian sea.
Our path is through the sky.
We have no time for sinners,
but only those who love to practise
what is good, holy and just:

it's those who are under our protection,
and we rescue them from their difficult trials.
As a god, I give you mortals good advice:
commit no crime,
and never sail with anyone who breaks his oath.

## CHORUS

Farewell: whoever can do that,
And keep free from mishap
Is a man who fares well indeed.

*Exeunt omnes.*

**Glossary and Pronunciation Guide**

ACHILLES (ah-KILL-eeze), greatest warrior of the Greeks.

AEGISTHUS (ee-GIS-thous), son of Thyestes, who fathered him on his daughter Pelopia. Atreus murdered Thyestes' children and served them up to him as cooked meat in an act of vengeance because of Thyestes' adulterous relationship with Atreus' wife, Aerope. Aegisthus swore to avenge his father on the son of Atreus, Agamemnon. After Agamemnon's murder, he married Clytemnestra. See THYESTES.

AGAMEMNON (AG-ah-MEM-non), son of Atreus, king of Argos, conqueror of Troy. Killed by Clytemnestra, his wife, after his return.

ALPHEUS (al-FEE-us), river in the Peloponnese.

APOLLO (ah-POL-oh), son of Zeus by Leto, brother to Artemis. He is the prophet god of Delphi, who sanctioned Orestes killing his mother.

ARCADIA (ar-CAY-dee-ah), country in the Peloponnese, noted for its rural charms.

ARES (AIR-reeze), son of Zeus and Hera, God of war.

ARGOS (ARE-gos), the names of Argos and Mycenae are often used interchangeably in Greek tragedy. Argos can refer to the city or the territory, the Argolid. Argive means coming from Argos.

ARTEMIS (ART-em-iss), daughter of Leto, sister to Apollo and virgin goddess of the hunt. She held back the winds at Aulis because Agamemnon slew her sacred stag and boasted about it. She is invoked by both Clytemnestra and Electra in this play. She is a god of women and helps them in childbirth. She also can be cruel in exacting vengeance.

ATHENA (ah-THEE-nah), goddess of wisdom and war, she was the patron goddess of Athens.

CASSANDRA (ca-SAN-drah), the mad priestess referred to in the play. A Trojan princess, and loved by Apollo, Agamemnon took her back to Mycenae from Troy as his personal prize. Because she had rejected Apollo's advances she was cursed with a gift of prophecy that no one would believe.

CLYTEMNESTRA (CLY-tem-NEEST-ra), daughter of Leda, sister of Helen, mother of Electra, Iphigenia, Orestes, and Chrysothemis. Sometimes we find the names Iphianassa and Laodice instead of Iphigenia or Electra. In this play, Clytemnestra protected both her children from Aegisthus' anger.

CYCLOPEAN WALLS, walls made with huge stones by the Cyclops (giants) for Argos.

DARDANUS (DAR-da-nus), builder of Troy's citadel who ruled over the Troad (region of Troy).

ELECTRA (e-LEK-tra), daughter of Clytemnestra and Agamemnon. She is called Laodice in Homer and that name means "Justice of the people."

ERINYS (ere-RINE-es), one of the Furies, goddess of vengeance (depicted by Aeschylus as having snakes instead of hair). Sophocles describes her as having bronze claws.

GORGON (GORE-gon), female monster with snake hair. Medusa was a gorgon, and her gaze could turn a person to stone.

HADES (HAY-deeze), god of the underworld, and also the name of the underworld itself. The god is married to Persephone, daughter of Demeter whom he stole from her mother. He shares her with Demeter: the flourishing months of spring and summer are when she is reunited with her mother, the goddess of grain.

HECTOR (HECK-tor), greatest warrior of Troy, married to Andromache.

HELEN, wife of Menelaus, brother of Agamemnon. She was abducted by Paris, prince of Troy, on whose account the Trojan War was fought.

HEPHAESTUS (hef-EYE-stus), god of fire, blacksmith-god and god of crafts.

HERA (HERE-rah), wife of Zeus and goddess of marriage.

HERMES (HER-meeze), son of Zeus and Maia, the messenger god, who is often shown carrying his caduceus, a staff, and wearing winged shoes. He sometimes wears the Helmet of Hades, which makes the wearer invisible. He is invoked in this play to conceal the plot until the proper time.

HILL OF ARES (Areopagus), a hill in Athens, northwest of the Acropolis where crimes for capital punishment were tried.

HYADES (HIGH-ah-dees), stars (formerly nymphs) in the constellation of the bull.

ILIUM (ILL-ee-um), another name for TROY.

IPHIANASSA (EYE-fee-ah-NASS-a), according to Homer, (*Il.* 9.145) another daughter of Agamemnon along with Chrysothemis, Laodice (or Electra), and Orestes. Iphianassa is sometimes identified with Iphigenia.

IPHIGENIA (if-ih-jen-EYE-ah), sister of Electra, sacrificed by Agamemnon at Aulis, following an oracle, so that he could sail to Troy.

MENELAUS (me-neh-LAY-us), king of Sparta and husband of Helen. Along with Agamemnon, one of the leaders of the expedition against Troy.

MYCENAE (my-SEE-nee), see ARGOS.

MYRTILUS (MYR-ti-lus), see PELOPS.

NAUPLIA (NOW-plee-ah), port in the Argolid.

NEREIDS (NEAR-ee-ids), sea-goddesses.

NIOBE (ni-OH-bee), daughter of Tantalus and sister of Pelops. She challenged Leto by sneering at her having only two children in comparison with her many (in tragedy about twenty). Those two (Apollo and Artemis) slew all her children. She was turned into a cliff (possibly on Mount Sipylus in Asia Minor) where she weeps endlessly, mourning her lost children.

OLYMPUS (oh-LIM-pus), mountain in Thessaly where the gods were said to live.

ORESTES (or-RES-teeze), son of Agamemnon and Clytemnestra, brother of Electra. He kills his mother in response to Apollo's oracle which commanded him to take vengeance for Agamemnon's murder.

PELOPONNESE (pel-o-po-NEES), large peninsula of southern Greece.

PELOPS (PEE-lops), son of Tantalus and uncle of Atreus and Thyestes. He cheated in a chariot race to win his bride, Hippodameia, and slew Myrtilus, the charioteer of Oenomaus (Hippodemeia's father), although he had been his ally. Some say that Pelops killed him to avoid paying Myrtilus the money he owed him for rigging Oenomaus' chariot so that Pelops could win.

PERSEUS (PER-see-us), son of Zeus and Danae. Slew Medusa and rescued Andromeda.

PHOCIS (FOE-kis), country of central Greece, near Mt. Parnassus.

PHOEBUS (FEE-bus), another name for APOLLO. It means "bright" or "shining."

PHRYGIANS (FRI-jee-ans), inhabitants of Phrygia, a country in Asia Minor. Troy was its most important city.

PLEIADES (PLEE-ah-dees), daughters of Atlas and Maia the mother of Hermes was one of them. They became a constellation in the sky.

POLYDEUCES (poly-DEW-seas), also known as Pollux, brother of Castor.

POSEIDON (puhs-EYE-don), god of the ocean and patron of Colonus.

**PROCNE** (PROCK-nee), who killed her child Itys to avenge herself on her husband Tereus who had raped her sister Philomela and cut out her tongue. But weaving the story in a tapestry, Philomela revealed to her sister Procne what had happened. Procne was turned into a nightingale who weeps forever, calling for her son Itys.

**PROTEUS** (PRO-tee-us), sea-god who could change shape at will.

**PYLADES** (PILE-ah-deeze), friend and companion of Orestes. He is the son of Strophius, the Phocian who provided a home for Orestes when he needed protection.

**SPHINX** (SFINKS), a monster: part woman, part lion with the wings of a bird of prey.

**STROPHIUS** (STROPH-ee-us), King of Phocis and father of PYLADES.

**TANTALUS** (TANT-ah-lus), king of Phrygia, son of Zeus, and father of Pelops. Punished for his crimes in Hades.

**THESSALIAN** (thess-AY-lee-an), inhabitant of Thessaly, northeast part of Greece, famous for horses.

**THETIS** (THEE-tis), sea-goddess, mother of Achilles (see NEREIDS and ACHILLES).

**THYESTES** (thy-EST-eeze), Atreus murdered and served him his own children to eat, without his knowing, out of vengeance for his wife's seduction by Thyestes. Thyestes swore vengeance and engendered a child on his own daughter, Pelopia. That child was Aegisthus.

**TROJAN WAR**, fought for ten years at Troy, under the leadership of Agamemnon. This war was waged because

Paris stole Helen away from Menelaus, the king of Sparta and brother of Menelaus. Helen's suitors had pledged to fight to recover her if she was ever stolen away from her husband.

**TROY,** City in northwest Asia Minor (see TROJAN WAR).

**TUTOR,** in the play the Old Man was Orestes' tutor, a slave to whom the care and education of Agamemnon and later the child Orestes were entrusted. He saw Orestes safely out of Argos when Aegisthus wanted to kill him, and brought him to Strophius in Phocis.

**TYNDAREUS** (tin-DAR-i-us), married to Leda, father of Helen, Clytemnestra, Castor and Polydeuces. Zeus is also said to have fathered Helen and Polydeuces (also known as Pollux).

**ZEUS** (ZYOOS), king of the gods.